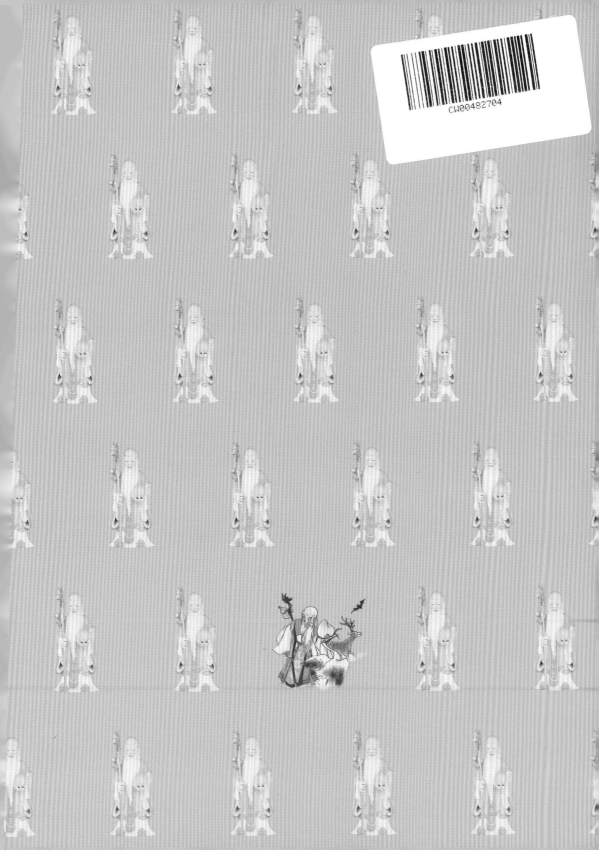

CW00482704

INTRIGUING

CHINESE
CULTURE 2

Y H MEW

 CHINA INTERCONTINENTAL PRESS

图书在版编目（CIP）数据

有趣的中国文化. 2：英文 / 苗耀华著.
-- 北京：五洲传播出版社，2016.10
（趣读中国文化系列）
ISBN 978-7-5085-3544-9

Ⅰ. ①有… Ⅱ. ①苗… Ⅲ. ①中华文化- 英文 Ⅳ. ①K203

中国版本图书馆CIP数据核字(2016)第226295号

Intriguing Chinese Culture 2

著　　　者：Y H Mew
出 版 人：荆孝敏
策划编辑：Lisa Zhang
责任编辑：王莉 张美景
装帧设计：宋索迪
出版发行：五洲传播出版社
地　　　址：北京市海淀区北三环中路31号生产力大楼B座6层
邮　　　编：100088
发行电话：010-82005927, 010-82007837
网　　　址：http://www.cicc.org.cn, http://www.thatsbooks.com
印　　　刷：恒美印务（广州）有限公司
版　　　次：2017年6月第1版 2017年6月第1次印刷
开　　　本：711×965mm 1/16
印　　　张：7.25
字　　　数：60千字
定　　　价：59.80元

Preface

This series is a general introduction to traditional Chinese
ideas and beliefs that are still relevant to present-day
Chinese practices. It is largely intended for non-Chinese
readers, as well as Chinese readers who are more
comfortable with the English language and who may have
just a smattering of understanding of Chinese culture.

Books on Chinese culture, especially those in the Chinese
language, are often written in a serious style and generally
demand some basic knowledge of the subject. The books
in this series have adopted instead a topical approach,
dealing with individual topics such as particular animals
and festivals, *feng shui*, colour, numbers, folk culture, and so
on, with the intention of bringing Chinese culture alive. A
number of the topics, such as dragon and bat, also provide
an interesting contrast between Western and Chinese
beliefs.

The series is generously illustrated to make reading easy.
Wherever possible, there is also a list of relevant Chinese
phrases and idioms with English translations to give readers
greater understanding of the topic concerned.

It is hoped that this series of books will help readers who
speak different languages better understand and appreciate
the cultures of others.

Contents

dog 狗 gǒu

Dogs have seldom been treated in China as man's best friend, as they are in the West.

In the Chinese language, most phrases or idioms relating to dogs are uncomplimentary. Paparazzi, for example, are referred to as 狗仔队 (gǒu zǎi duì), literally 'a team of little dogs'.

Eating of dog's meat in China dates back over 2,000 years. In northern and parts of southern China, some people still eat dog's meat, believing that it will keep them warm in winter. The expression 挂羊头卖狗肉 (guà yáng tóu mài gǒu ròu), literally 'hanging a goat's head but selling dog's meat', means to deceive.

Today, partly because of Western influence and partly because of greater affluence, more families in China keep dogs as pets and many people have spoken out against the habit of eating dog's meat. Hopefully, dogs can now enjoy a better life in China.

Idioms and phrases

狗胆包天 gǒu dǎn bāo tiān
to have the audacity

狗急跳墙 gǒu jí tiào qiáng
in desperation

狗屁 gǒu pì
(a rather rude phrase) nonsense

狗屁不通 gǒu pì bù tōng
(of speech or writing) unreadable; nonsense

狗头军师 gǒu tóu jūn shī
a bad adviser

狗腿子 gǒu tuǐ zi
henchman

狗熊 gǒu xióng
a common name for a black bear; a coward

狗眼看人低 gǒu yǎn kàn rén dī
to be snobbish; to look down on others

狗仗人势 gǒu zhàng rén shì
literally 'a dog is fierce because of the backing of its master'; often used to refer to the bullying tactics of the subordinates of a powerful boss

狗嘴里吐不出象牙
gǒu zuǐ lǐ tǔ bù chū xiàng yá
Since it is impossible for a dog's mouth to produce ivory, one should never expect something worthwhile from a worthless person.

door gods 门神 mén shén

Door gods have been known in Chinese culture for a long time. From the Han dynasty onwards, people hired artists to paint portraits of legendary fierce-looking warriors on their doors to ward off evil spirits. These legendary figures were later worshipped as door gods, because people believed that they were feared by evil spirits.

In the Tang dynasty, these legendary figures were replaced by historical personalities such as Qin Shubao and Yu Chigong, who were generals under the second emperor, Taizong. It was said that the emperor was much disturbed in his sleep by the Dragon King, so he decided to get his two famous generals painted on the palace doors. Thereafter, apparently no evil spirit dared to come near him.

In the late Tang dynasty, some people also painted the famous 'ghost-catcher' Zhong Kui on their doors, and worshipped him as a door god.

The concept of the door gods underwent further changes in later years. In the Song dynasty, people also painted images of famous officials on their doors. In addition to warding off evil spirits, these portraits served as decorations.

Idioms and phrases

门户 mén hù
door

门可罗雀 mén kě luó què
literally 'one can catch sparrows at the doorstep', signifying that a shop does not have many customers

门口 mén kǒu
door

门铃 mén líng
doorbell

门牌 mén pái
house number

门市店 mén shì diàn
retail shop

门庭若市 mén tíng ruò shì
a very busy shop

Double Nine Festival

重阳节 chóng yáng jié

In Chinese culture, the ninth day of the ninth month of the lunar calendar is called the Double Nine Festival. It is known in Chinese as either 'Double Nine' 重九 (chóng jiǔ) or 'Double Yang' 重阳 (chóng yáng). The latter name is, however, more common, because nine is a *yang* number.

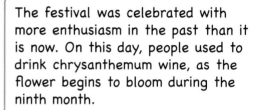

The festival was celebrated with more enthusiasm in the past than it is now. On this day, people used to drink chrysanthemum wine, as the flower begins to bloom during the ninth month.

There also used to be a custom among the Chinese to go mountain climbing during this festival, as it marks the beginning of the autumn season, when the weather is good for such outings.

The mountain-climbing tradition has its roots in a Taoist story about a man being advised by his master to take his family to a mountain in order to escape from a bad spirit.

Idioms and phrases

重 chóng
> to duplicate or repeat

重播 chóng bō
> repeat telecast or broadcast

重操旧业 chóng cāo jiù yè
> to do the same trade again

重蹈覆辙 chóng dǎo fù zhé
> to fall into the same trap again

重返 chóng fǎn
> to return to the same place

重犯 chóng fàn
> to repeat an offence or mistake

重逢 chóng féng
> to meet again

重复 chóng fù
> to repeat

重见天日 chóng jiàn tiān rì
> literally 'to see the light of the day again', meaning to be able to live a new life

重建 chóng jiàn
> to reconstruct or rebuild

重提 chóng tí
> to bring up the same issue again

重新做人 chóng xīn zuò rén
> (of an offender) to turn over a new leaf

重修旧好 chóng xiū jiù hǎo
> to let bygones be bygones and become friends again

dowry 嫁妆 jià zhuāng

The dowry used to be an important part of Asian culture in general. In India, in particular, it remains so important that young women who do not have a decent dowry when they get married may still be ill-treated by their in-laws. Occasionally, this can even lead to a tragic end.

In China, the dowry also used to be an important institution. Before a woman was married, her parents would normally give her presents such as gold, jade and a camphor chest. The value of the dowry that she brought to the husband's family would be an indication of the wealth of her family; the more it was, the greater her status.

This could be the reason behind the traditional emphasis on match-making couples whose families had comparable economic and social status. This was known as 门当户对 (mén dāng hù duì).

Although the dowry is still part and parcel of the events surrounding a wedding ceremony, it is practised today more in token form. No reasonable in-laws will take pride in the amount of dowry brought by the daughter-in-law.

Idioms and phrases

嫁鸡随鸡, 嫁狗随狗 jià jī suí jī jià gǒu suí gǒu

literally 'when a woman was married to a rooster, she had to follow the rooster; when she was married to a dog, she had to follow the dog'. This is an old Chinese saying that reveals the low social status of women in former times – she had to follow whoever she was married to, however poor the man was.

嫁娶 jià qǔ

In the Chinese language, 嫁 (jià) means 'a woman marries a man'. 娶 (qǔ) means 'a man marries a woman'.

嫁人 jià rén

(of a woman) to be married

dragon 龙 lóng

The dragon, one of the 12 animals of the Chinese zodiac, is a legendary animal in both the West and the East. In Western folklore, the dragon is often depicted as a fire-spitting monster that symbolizes evil and eventually dies by the sword of a brave knight.

In the East, however, the dragon is considered an auspicious creature.

According to legend, the dragon had nine sons, all with very rare names that almost defy pronunciation. They not only looked different but were also assigned different functions. The phrase 龙生九子 (lóng shēng jiǔ zǐ) therefore also means that children from the same parents may be different in look and ability.

Bixi 赑屃 (bì xì) , one of the sons of the dragon

In traditional Chinese belief, the dragon resided in the sea, in a palace called the 'Dragon's Palace', and was responsible for casting rain. He was worshipped all over the country in temples called the 'Dragon's Temple'. People would go there to pray for all sorts of things, especially for rain when there was a drought.

In Chinese history and culture, the dragon was always associated with the emperor. The imperial throne was known as the 'dragon's chair'. The emperor's body was referred to as the 'dragon's body' and his robe, which was embroidered with the images of nine dragons, was called the 'dragon's robe'. If the empress or concubine was pregnant, she was said to be bearing the 'dragon's seed'.

As the Chinese view the dragon as auspicious, in countries where there is a sizeable Chinese community, people still perform the dragon dance during certain festivals, such as the Lunar New Year.

In the Year of the Dragon, the birth rate among the Chinese is usually higher than in other years, indicating that Chinese parents still believe that the Year of the Dragon is a good year to have babies.

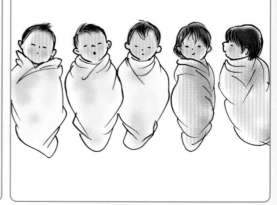

And it is perhaps the aspiration of all Chinese parents that one day their sons will bring honour to their family, hence the saying 'wishing the son to become a dragon' 望子成龙 (wàng zǐ chéng lóng).

Idioms and phrases

龙船 lóng chuán
> dragon boat

龙凤呈祥 lóng fèng chéng xiáng
> literally 'the dragon and phoenix present good luck'; a phrase often used in the Lunar New Year to wish for good luck

龙卷风 lóng juǎn fēng
> tornado

龙潭虎穴 lóng tán hǔ xué
> literally 'the dragon's pool and the tiger's den', meaning a very dangerous place

龙头 lóng tóu
> literally 'the dragon's head', meaning the leader in something

龙虾 lóng xiā
> lobster

龙争虎斗 lóng zhēng hǔ dòu
> literally 'a fierce fight between a dragon and a tiger'; a well-matched fight

龙舟 lóng zhōu
> the dragon boat, which is used in competition during the Dragon Boat Festival on the fifth day of the fifth month of the lunar calendar.

Dragon Boat Festival
端午节 duān wǔ jié

The Dragon Boat Festival is known as 端午节 (duān wǔ jié) in the Chinese language. Among the notable features of this festival is the eating of triangular-shaped dumplings 粽子 (zòng zi) made with glutinous rice, with or without fillings.

The festival had its origins more than 2000 years ago, in the Warring States period in Chinese history. It commemorates the death of Qu Yuan, a patriotic poet in the court of the King of Chu. As he was not able to persuade the king to mend his ways after numerous attempts, and finding himself being distanced by other officials, he committed suicide by jumping into the Miluo River on the fifth day of the fifth month of the lunar calendar.

On hearing the sad news, the people of Chu boarded their boats to look for the poet's body, without success. In order to prevent his body being eaten by sea creatures, they cooked rice wrapped in bamboo leaves and threw them into the river to distract the fish.

Nowadays, in addition to eating dumplings, the festival is often celebrated with a dragon-boat race on the river. The dragon boats themselves are decorated with a dragon's head at the bow and a dragon's tail at the stern.

dreams 梦 mèng

The Chinese believed that there was a close relationship between dreams and reality. Dreams were often used to interpret what was going to happen. For example, if a person dreamed of a bear, it was believed that his wife would give birth to a son.

According to legend, before the Goddess of the Sea Ma-zu was born, her mother dreamed of the Goddess of Mercy Guan-yin. Guan-yin gave her a pill that would help her to give birth to a female 'saint'. When Ma-zu's mother woke up, she found the pill by her side.

In the story *The Magic Paint Brush* a poor boy Ma Liang dreams of an old man who gives him a paint brush. When he wakes up, much to his surprise, he finds the brush by his side. He uses it to paint a lot of things that come miraculously to life. By so doing he is able to help the poor around him by painting what they need.

One of the most famous dreams is that described in *The Magic Pillow*, which was written during the Tang dynasty. This story tells of a poor scholar who has failed his exams. One day, in an inn, the scholar meets a Taoist priest who lends him a porcelain pillow.

When the scholar sleeps on it, he dreams that he has become a high official and enjoys all kinds of luxury in the imperial court. But when he wakes up from his dream, all the riches and honours disappear, and he is just the same poor scholar. This is known as 黄粱梦 (huáng liáng mèng).

In popular Chinese culture, one often reads about ghosts appearing in the dreams of their family members in order to convey a message. This is known as 托梦 (tuō mèng).

Idioms and phrases

梦话 mèng huà
> words spoken when one is asleep

梦幻 mèng huàn
> a dream; an illusion

梦见 mèng jiàn
> to dream of someone or something

梦境 mèng jìng
> in a dream; in dreamland

梦寐以求 mèng mèi yǐ qiú
> to crave for something even in one's dreams

梦游 mèng yóu
> to sleepwalk

duck 鸭 yā

Visitors to China, especially to Beijing, would not want to miss the famous Peking Roast Duck 北京烤鸭 (běi jīng kǎo yā). This roast duck dish is now widely available in various Chinese restaurants around the world.

Some people also have a special liking for braised duck's feet. In Taiwan of China, there is a popular dish called Ginger Duck, in which ginger is cooked with duck in a stew. This dish is usually eaten during winter.

dumpling 饺子 jiǎo zi

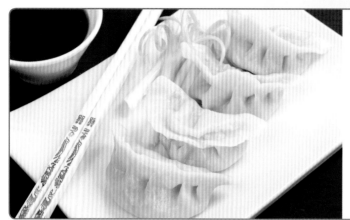

The dumpling is a traditional staple food of the Chinese in northern China.

Dumplings are made by wrapping meat and vegetables in pieces of thin dough. They come in different shapes and sizes. Dumplings can be steamed, boiled or fried.

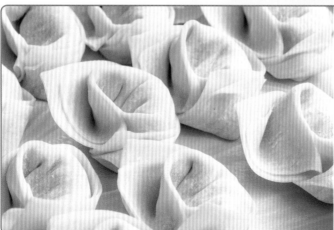

Dumplings can be shaped like ancient gold or silver ingots, which is why they are considered auspicious.

It is common for a family in northern China to make dumplings together on the eve of the Lunar New Year. This tradition is supposed to bring good luck to the family.

It is customary, while making dumplings, to put a small coin in one of them. It is believed that whoever finds the coin while eating the dumplings will enjoy good fortune for the rest of the year.

eight 八 bā

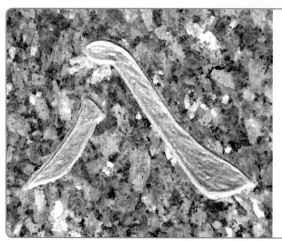

The number eight is considered a very lucky number in Chinese culture, because it sounds like 发 (fā) or 'to prosper' in some Chinese dialects and in Mandarin. Hence, Chinese people generally love this number.

Car numbers with the digit 8 are popular among the Chinese. Some people would spend lots of money bidding for them.

E 1888 Y

The number is such a favourite that during festive seasons retailers and restaurants commonly set prices containing this number. For example, a pot of kumquat plant may cost $88 and a set meal for six diners may cost $888.

The Beijing Olympics began on 8 August 2008. To make the timing even more auspicious, the games were officially declared open at eight minutes and eight seconds past eight in the evening.

Idioms and phrases

八成 bā chéng
80 percent

八方 bā fāng
from all directions

八角形 bā jiǎo xíng
octagon

八九不离十 bā jiǔ bù lí shí
very close

八面玲珑 bā miàn líng lóng
able to deal with people in a smooth and slick way

八面威风 bā miàn wēi fēng
awesome

八仙 bā xiān
the Eight Immortals in Chinese folklore

八月 bā yuè
August

八字没一撇 bā zì méi yī piě
still on the drawing board

Eight Immortals 八仙 bā xiān

The Eight Immortals of Taoist origin are popular figures in Chinese folk culture. They are Han Zhongli, Zhang Guolao, Lu Dongbin, Li Tieguai, Han Xiangzi, Cao Guojiu, Lan Caihe and He Xiangu. He Xiangu is the only female amongst the Immortals.

There have been different versions of their origins and exactly who the Eight Immortals were. By the time of the Ming dynasty, the names of the Eight Immortals had been established once and for all by the writer of a book called *Travel to the East*.

The Eight Immortals are said to represent men, women, the old, the young, the rich and the poor. Before they achieved immortality, they were just ordinary people with human weaknesses. The fact that ordinary people too could achieve immortality made them more appealing to the common folk.

Each of the Eight Immortals has their own magic tool. And the Chinese saying 八仙过海, 各显神通 (bā xiān guò hǎi，gè xiǎn shén tōng), literally 'like the Eight Immortals crossing the sea, each employing their own skill'), is often quoted when there is no prior agreed plan about doing something, and each individual is left to their own devices.

The Eight Immortals are a symbol of prosperity and longevity. Paintings or murals of them were often seen on the walls of houses of the rich. Their statues and paintings, either alone or in a group, are as popular today as in the past since they are a symbol of good luck.

elephant 象 xiàng

Elephants are known to have been used in battle in some countries, but never in China, although the animal has been present in the country for a long time.

In the 3rd century AD, Cao Cao, the ruler of the state of Wei, was given an elephant and wanted to find out its weight. While all his officials were at their wits' end, his son Cao Chong, then only five years old, came up with an idea. He asked the officials to drive the animal onto a boat then mark the water level.

The elephant was then driven from the boat and the officials were instructed to fill it with boulders until the boat reached the same water level. That way, they finally worked out the weight of the elephant by weighing the boulders. Cao Cao was naturally impressed by his son's ingenuity.

The elephant is an endangered animal, mainly because of its tusks. For centuries, the Chinese people have displayed great skill in making objects from ivory, a tough material derived from the tusks of elephants. Ivory objects such as vases, bangles, chains and chopsticks used to be made by skilful craftsmen in Southeast Asia.

This lucrative trade led to the killing of numerous elephants for their tusks. Since the 1990s, there has been an international ban on ivory products, which has put a damper on the ivory trade.

13

elixir 长生药 cháng shēng yào

Longevity is a traditional symbol of good luck in China and it is hardly surprising that many people, especially emperors, should take a strong interest in prolonging their life or even trying to overcome death through the use of elixirs.

One way of trying to achieve longevity was to consume pills of immortality. These pills were usually made by alchemists, using a special three-legged cauldron, either in the palace grounds or secluded places in the mountains. Alchemy was closely associated with Taoism, which became popular in the latter part of the Han dynasty.

It was believed that a person taking pills of immortality would not only become immortal but would also have the power to turn iron into gold. Various emperors in the Han, Tang, Ming and Qing dynasties resorted to achieving immortality this way, but to no avail. Some even died of poisoning.

People formerly also believed that there existed a species of plant that had the quality of immortality. This plant was later identified as the *lingzhi* 灵芝 (líng zhī), a type of fungus, much valued by the Chinese people for its health qualities.

According to the great Han dynasty historian Sima Qian, the first emperor of China, Qin Shi Huang, dispatched an alchemist Xu Fu together with a few thousand children to look for the plant overseas. The mission obviously failed, as the emissary never returned.

In the *Legend of the White Snake*
《白蛇传》 (bái shé zhuàn), the
scholar Xu Xian dies of shock after
seeing his wife change into a huge
snake. To save her husband, the
White Snake goes to Mount Kunlun
to steal the *lingzhi*, and revives
him.

While searching for immortal plants over
the centuries, other plants were accidentally
discovered to be of value to people's health.
One of these was ginseng 人参 (rén shēn).

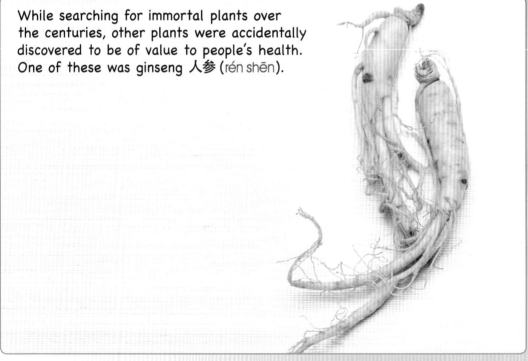

emperor/empress
皇帝/皇后 huáng dì / huáng hòu

Before the Qin dynasty, in the 3rd century BC, the earlier rulers of China such as those of the Shang dynasty and the Zhou dynasty, went by the title of 'king'. After the unification of China in 221 BC, however, Chinese rulers adopted the title of 'emperor'.

King Wu of Zhou dynasty

The founding emperor of the Qin dynasty wanted his empire to last a long time, and called himself the First Emperor. In fact, his empire lasted barely 15 years after the death of his son, the Second Emperor.

Qin Shi Huang, the first emperor of China

Chinese emperors considered themselves to be the Son of Heaven and to have unlimited powers, since heaven was viewed with the deepest respect by almost everyone. The emperors came to adopt the dragon as a symbol of their authority, so such phrases as the 'dragon's chair' (that is, the throne), the 'dragon's body' and the 'dragon's robe' are all related to the emperor.

The number nine and the number five used to refer to the emperor or the imperial throne. This is because of the odd numbers from one to nine, nine (九) (jiǔ) is the largest and five (五) (wǔ) is at the centre, so both nine and five constituted appropriate references to the emperor since he was the centre of power and the highest in authority.

Emperor Taizong of Tang dynasty

The first wife of the emperor was the empress. Her first son, the crown prince, would often succeed the throne after the emperor died, even though he might still be a minor. In such cases the empress-dowager might be present at audiences but remained behind a screen.

It was common for the emperor to have numerous concubines in his harem. Concubines had different rankings and titles. Occasionally, a concubine might gain imperial favour, for example the famous Yang Guifei of the Tang dynasty. With so many concubines and children by them, it was no surprise that there were many court intrigues.

Yang Guifei

Chinese emperors called themselves *zhen* 朕(zhèn) or *gua ren* 寡人(guǎ rén). The empress used the name *ai jia* 哀家(āi jiā). Officials would address the emperor as His Majesty, or Ten Thousand Years, and it was common practice for them to kneel on both knees before the emperor as a sign of respect.

During the Qing dynasty, the last of the Chinese dynasties, officials sometimes called themselves 'slaves' 奴才(nú cái). Officials in earlier Chinese dynasties would normally address themselves as *chen* 臣 (chén).

Idioms and phrases

皇储 *huáng chǔ*

crown prince; the same as **皇太子** (huáng tài zǐ)

皇冠 *huáng guān*

crown

皇宫 *huáng gōng*

palace

皇家 *huáng jiā*

imperial household

皇亲国戚 *huáng qīn guó qì*

imperial relatives

皇权 *huáng quán*

imperial power

皇上 *huáng shàng*

emperor

皇室 *huáng shì*

imperial family

皇太后 *huáng tài hòu*

empress-dowager; mother of the reigning emperor

皇位 *huáng wèi*

throne

皇族 *huáng zú*

imperial clan

15

euphemism 婉辞 wǎn cí

The Chinese language, like many other languages, has various euphemisms that are commonly used in daily life. For example, when a person dies, the common English euphemism is that he or she has 'passed away'. The Chinese refer to a person's death as 'everlasting sleep' 永眠(yǒng mián) or sometimes 'after one hundred years' 百年之后(bǎi nián zhī hòu).

In obituaries, common euphemisms are 'immortal death' 仙逝(xiān shì), 'riding the crane to the west' 驾鹤西归 (jià hè xī guī, the west is associated with paradise), 'to leave behind a good name forever' 万古流芳(wàn gǔ liú fāng).

Euphemisms referring to the death of an emperor were different. An emperor's death would be referred to as *jia beng* 驾崩(jià bēng). When the abbot of a temple dies, he is said to have *zuo hua* 坐化(zuò huà) or *yuan ji* 圆寂(yuán jì).

The Chinese often use the word 'long life' to refer to things associated with the dead. For example, the coffin is called 'the long-life wood' or 'long-life planks' 寿板(shòu bǎn), the clothes worn by the dead are called 'long-life clothes' 寿衣(shòu yī), and so on. 'Red and white business' 红白事 (hóng bái shì) refers to services associated in general with weddings ('red') and funerals ('white').

When a soldier is wounded in a war, he is said 'to hang decorations' 挂彩(guà cǎi).

If someone tells tales about their colleagues, especially their mistakes, to the boss, that person is said to be 'making a small report' 打小报告(dǎ xiǎo bào gào).

Chicken feet are a delicacy to many Chinese, especially the Cantonese. In restaurants selling *dim sum* 点心(diǎn xīn), however, chicken feet are known as 'phoenix claws' 凤爪(fèng zhǎo).

In the Chinese language, when you want to go to the toilet, you can say you want to go to the 'room for washing hands' 洗手间(xǐ shǒu jiān) or to the 'hygiene room' 卫生间(wèi shēng jiān) or to the 'powder room' 化妆室 (化妝室) (huà zhuāng shì).

When a business fails and has to be wrapped up, the euphemism is 关门大吉(guān mén dà jí), which means, literally, 'close the door for good luck'.

In the past, women did not want to tell their husbands or family that they were pregnant. Instead, they would say 'I have got it' 我有了(wǒ yǒu le).

'Black gold' 黑金(hēi jīn) is a euphemism used to refer to money made from corruption or other illegal activities, such as extortion. In a country where politicians are involved in such practices, people talk of 'black gold politics' 黑金政治(hēi jīn zhèng zhì).

face 面子/脸 miàn zi / liǎn

The face, known in the Chinese language either as *mian* 面(miàn) or *lian* 脸(liǎn) has always had great significance in Chinese culture. In this context, the word is associated with one's dignity and social standing and not the physical attractiveness.

A person who has done something despicable may be accused by others for 'not wanting his or her face' 不要脸(bù yào liǎn).

If a person 'loses face' 丢脸 (diū liǎn), it means they look foolish and have brought about dishonour not only to themselves but also to their family. They lose credibility and respect.

Since the Chinese generally care a lot about their 'face', they are often careful in what they say or do for fear of making mistakes. For example, students may be reluctant to respond to their teachers' questions, for fear of looking foolish when they give the wrong answers.

Idioms and phrases

面不改色　miàn bù gǎi sè
> literally 'the face does not change colour', meaning the person is very calm

面具　miàn jù
> mask

面貌　miàn mào
> the appearance; the facial features

面目　miàn mù
> literally 'face and eyes', meaning face

面目全非　miàn mù quán fēi
> beyond recognition

脸孔　liǎn kǒng
> face; the same as **面孔**(miàn kǒng)

脸皮　liǎn pí
> literally 'the skin of the face'. If someone's face is 'thin' **脸皮薄**(liǎn pí báo), they are sensitive and blush easily. If their face is 'thick' **脸皮厚**(liǎn pí hòu) or **厚脸皮**(hòu liǎn pí), they are insensitive and have no sense of shame.

脸色　liǎn sè
> the colour of the face; complexion

脸上无光　liǎn shàng wú guāng
> literally 'the face has no lustre'; to lose face

family 家庭 jiā tíng

In Confucian societies, the family is the basic social unit, the building block of society, unlike in the West where individuals are given more importance.

Traditionally, the father was the undisputed head of the family. He was usually the sole breadwinner and, generally, was occupied with the 'external affairs' and bigger issues affecting the family.

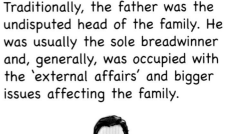

The mother used to be a full-time housewife, attending to the daily chores of the family, manning the kitchen, cooking, washing and looking after the children and her husband's parents, if they lived with them.

With greater social mobility, and ever-increasing demands for material comfort, however, the roles of both husband and wife have changed. It is now common for both husband and wife to work in order to earn enough money to raise their family.

For some families, it is also necessary to employ a domestic helper to do household chores and look after the children or the elderly. Increasingly, couples prefer to have a home of their own instead of living with their parents.

Idioms and phrases

家产　jiā chǎn

family property

家丑不可外扬　jiā chǒu bù kě wài yáng

don't wash the dirty linen in public

家传秘方　jiā chuán mì fāng

a secret family recipe handed down from one generation to the next

家家有本难念的经　jiā jiā yǒu běn nán niàn de jīng

every family has its problems

家破人亡　jiā pò rén wáng

a broken family, mainly as a result of a natural disaster or war

家人　jiā rén

the members of a family; the same as **家属**(jiā shǔ)

家务　jiā wù

household chores

family tree 家谱 jiā pǔ

In traditional China, it was usual for every family to have a book in which was recorded the genealogy of the family as far back as it could be traced. For the clan, there was the clan record, which was usually kept by the most senior member of the clan.

The family tree often recorded the male members alone, as traditional Chinese society was largely male-dominated. Female members may have their maiden family names recorded.

It is quite common nowadays for the descendants of those who migrated overseas in search of a better life to go back to China to search for their roots. The family tree, as well as the clan genealogy, can provide useful information about the extended family.

fan 扇子 shàn zi

The fan was an item carried especially by young scholars in the past, chiefly as a fashion accessory. Fans used by men were generally collapsible. Women, mainly from rich and scholarly families, also used fans but these were usually round in shape.

The fans were often decorated with paintings and it was not uncommon for poets or painters to write a poem or paint a picture on them.

Not all fans carried by scholars could be folded, however. During the Three Kingdoms period in the 3rd century AD, the famous strategist Zhu-ge Liang carried his trademark 'feather fan' that made him look confident and wise.

In the novel *Journey to the West* 《西游记》(xī yóu jì), which was written during the Ming dynasty in the 16th century, when the Buddhist monk Tang Sanzang and his three disciples came to the Flaming Mountains, the place was ablaze and they could not cross it.

Sun Wukong, also known as the Monkey King, the eldest disciple, managed to trick Princess Iron Fan, the wife of Bull King, to part with her magic 'palm-leaf fan'. He then used it to put out the blaze and they continued with their journey.

fate 命/命运 mìng / mìng yùn

Early civilizations all over the world believed that there was a force from heaven that controlled what happened on earth. Confucius once said that one's life and death was determined by fate, and that heaven would decide whether a person would be rich or poor.

At the end of the Qin dynasty, Liu Bang and Xiang Yu both aspired to succeed the empire. When it became clear to Xiang Yu that he was losing the fight, he cried out that it was heaven's will that he should fail. He eventually committed suicide.

In the *Romance of the Three Kingdoms* 《三国演义》(sān guó yǎn yì), the strategist Zhu-ge Liang knew that if his master Liu Bei wanted to succeed the Han dynasty, he had to eliminate his contender Cao Cao. But when Zhu-ge Liang observed the movements in the night sky, he concluded that Cao Cao was not destined to die.

So, although Cao Cao was cornered, he was eventually let go by Guan Gong, one of Liu Bei's ablest generals, who was sent to capture him. This episode, which dramatizes the capturing of Cao Cao and subsequently releasing him, is a popular theme in Beijing opera.

From the earliest times, people believed that one's fate was determined by the year, month, day and hour when one was born. This was also the basis for checking out whether a couple were compatible for marriage.

However, some people also believe that rather than moaning and groaning about one's fate and destiny, it is important to do your best and then leave it to heaven to decide if you are going to be successful or not.

In contemporary China, people are familiar with the idea of drawing lots to decide who should do something first, for example in a football match. People who believe in fate may go to temples to divine by 'drawing lots' on how things will turn out in relation to their career, marriage, luck, wealth, exams, etc.

Drawing lots for the purposes of divination is a common practice amongst the Chinese and the Japanese. The lots themselves are bamboo sticks, which have a corresponding message written on a piece of paper. This is supposed to communicate the divine will of the gods about a person's fate.

Some people in the past obviously believed that education might change their fate. If they passed an important imperial exam, for instance, they could become an official and not only their own life but also that of their immediate family and the entire clan could be improved.

In modern times, some people buy bamboo with stems that have been deliberately twisted for display at home during the Lunar New Year. The twisting of the bamboo stems signifies that one's fortune in the New Year will change for the better.

feng shui 风水 fēng shuǐ

Feng shui or geomancy has been practised for a long time in China. Literally, the phrase means 'wind', which refers to 'qi', or energy, and 'water', which signifies 'movement'. In other words, it is about the harmony between humans and nature. When harmony is achieved between humans and the surrounding environment, the people living there will be lucky and evil can be avoided.

Belief in *feng shui* can be traced back to more than 2,000 years ago in China. In its earlier days it was connected with choosing auspicious locations for palaces, houses and graveyards.

During the anti-foreign Boxer Rebellion in 1899–1901, the introduction of railways and other constructions in China were blamed for damaging the *feng shui* of the sites where they were built. To the Chinese, *feng shui* was important because it was supposed to have an impact on the living and future generations of a family.

Feng shui masters look at the *feng shui* of a place by using a special magnetic compass.

Houses built on high ground – for example, a hill – and facing a stretch of water are considered to have good *feng shui*. Likewise, the *feng shui* of a grave sited on high ground facing water is considered good.

To many sceptics, *feng shui* is just superstition. However, there are also firm believers, including non-Chinese. More and more Western companies in Asia, for example Hong Kong of China and Singapore, take local cultures and beliefs into consideration before constructing their buildings. Sometimes, on the advice of *feng shui* masters, they may even change the orientation of the entrance to their buildings, for example, in order to attract good luck to their business.

#20-14

Idioms and phrases

风波　fēng bō

literally 'wind and waves'; sometimes used metaphorically to signify disturbance

风吹雨打　fēng chuī yǔ dǎ

battered by wind and rain

风和日丽　fēng hé rì lì

a gentle breeze and a sunny day

风浪　fēng làng

the wind and the waves; sometimes used to describe the trying times in one's life

风平浪静　fēng píng làng jìng

literally 'the wind has stopped and the waves are quiet', meaning calm or uneventful

风扇　fēng shàn

electric fan

风声　fēng shēng

the sound of the wind; rumour; information

风云人物　fēng yún rén wù

man of the hour

filial piety 孝 xiào

Filial piety is one of the main Confucian virtues, along with patriotism, benevolence and righteousness. The concept is espoused in the *Classic of Filial Piety*.

In the classical sense, filial piety means being obedient and respectful to one's parents and grandparents, looking after them in their lifetime and observing the necessary rituals and sacrificial ceremonies to them in their afterlife. This is linked to the Chinese concept of 'repaying' – that is, to repay years of parental love and upbringing.

Filial piety as a concept continues to be widely acknowledged among the Chinese, regardless of education, religious belief or dialect group. Children are still taught from a young age to be filial to their elders. Indeed, traditionally, the Chinese believed that filial piety was the origin of all good deeds.

Famous stories about great acts of filial piety in the past are recorded in the *Twenty-four Filial Exemplars*, although these are now regarded as largely irrelevant by modern generations.

In traditional Chinese society, a person would be considered lacking in filial piety if they did not remonstrate with their parents when they were in the wrong; if they failed to take up employment to support their parents; and if they failed to get married in order to continue the family line. Of these three things, the failure to get married and to produce a male heir was considered the most serious fault of a man.

Idioms and phrases

孝道   xiào dào

     filial obligation or duty

孝敬   xiào jìng

     to behave with filial piety or duty

孝顺   xiào shùn

     to be filial

孝心   xiào xīn

     filial thoughts

23

the first birthday
抓周 zhuā zhōu

The celebration of the first birthday of a child has been an accepted practice amongst the Chinese people for about 2,000 years, ever since the Three Kingdoms period.

On the day itself, the traditional custom was to put a number of objects in a tray – such as a seal, a Chinese brush, an ink-stone, a book, an abacus, coins and sweets – for the child to pick up. Whichever object the child selected was meant to reveal what his interests would be when he grew up. If the child was a girl, other objects might be added.

If the child picked up a book, it meant he would likely be good at his studies; if he picked up the seal, he would probably end up being an imperial official – and so on. If a baby girl picked up a ruler (for measuring), it would be concluded that she would prove good at managing the household in the future.

In the *Dream of the Red Chamber*, a well-known novel written in the middle of the 18th century during the Qing dynasty, when the protagonist Jia Baoyu celebrates his first birthday, his father puts various things on a tray before him. The child picks up items associated with women, such as a comb and powder. Needless to say, his father is very unhappy, thinking that when the child grows up he will become a lecher. Although that is not the case, Jia Baoyu does prove to be fond of the company of girls.

This ancient practice is followed less often today than it used to be. When it is observed, it is usually in a spirit of fun and the items placed before the child are more likely to include such things as a computer mouse, a credit card and a calculator.

fish 鱼 yú

Fish have considerable cultural significance amongst the Chinese people. As the word 鱼 sounds like another Chinese character 余(yú) meaning 'extra' or 'surplus', fish have come to represent 'plentiful' or having more than enough of everything in daily life.

Many people eat fish during the Lunar New Year, especially at the reunion dinner on the Eve, in the belief that this will ensure their good fortune in the months ahead. This is called 年年有"余" (nián nián yǒu yú) or 连年有"余" (lián nián yǒu yú).

The goldfish has been known in China for more than 1,000 years and has long been a favourite choice of pet fish. They do not need a lot of space and can be kept in aquariums or fish bowls. Their golden colour is considered by the Chinese as a symbol of good luck. Today, there is a great variety of species of goldfish.

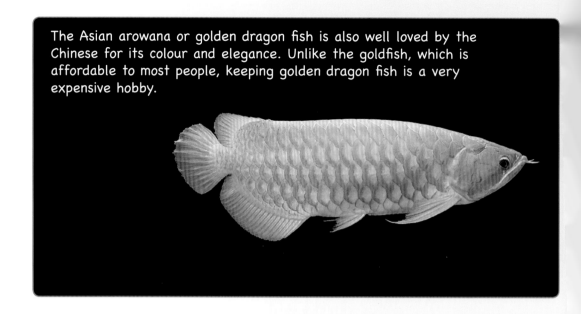

The Asian arowana or golden dragon fish is also well loved by the Chinese for its colour and elegance. Unlike the goldfish, which is affordable to most people, keeping golden dragon fish is a very expensive hobby.

Idioms and phrases

鱼饵　yú ěr
bait

鱼缸　yú gāng
aquarium, fish bowl

鱼米之乡　yú mǐ zhī xiāng
a place where fish and rice abound

鱼目混珠　yú mù hùn zhū
literally 'fish eyes and pearls are jumbled up', meaning not knowing good from bad

鱼肉　yú ròu
fish meat

鱼水情　yú shuǐ qíng
close relations, like fish and water

鱼子酱　yú zǐ jiàng
caviar

five 五 wǔ

In ancient China, it was believed that the number five was in the middle of the yang (odd) numbers, namely one, three, five, seven and nine. Since nine is the biggest of these numbers and five is at the centre, the two numbers were used to refer to the emperor or the imperial throne.

Idioms and phrases

五边形 wǔ biān xíng
    pentagon

五彩缤纷 wǔ cǎi bīn fēn
    colourful

五花八门 wǔ huā bā mén
    a great variety

五星级 wǔ xīng jí
    (of hotels) five-star

五颜六色 wǔ yán liù sè
    multi-coloured

五月 wǔ yuè
    May

五岳 wǔ yuè
    the Five Mountains

五指 wǔ zhǐ
    the five fingers

五洲 wǔ zhōu
    literally 'the five continents'; referring to the whole world

the five elements
五行 wǔ xíng

The five elements represent an ancient Chinese view of the universe in which it was believed that nature was made up of metal, wood, water, fire and earth. Ancient Chinese philosophers used these five elements to explain the origins of everything on earth.

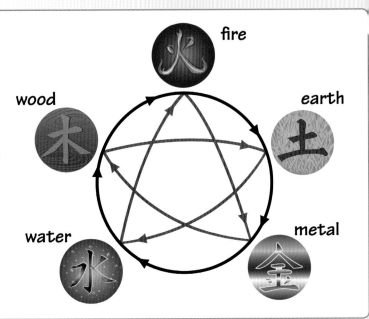

fire

wood

earth

water

metal

Traditional Chinese medicine uses the five elements to explain the nature of the human body. For example, if a person lacks a certain element, they are likely to suffer from a certain illness.

Diviners used the compatibility and incompatibility of the five elements to explain the workings of fate.

the five kinds of luck
五福 wǔ fú

According to traditional Chinese belief, there are five kinds of luck that are probably the greatest blessings a person can ever aspire to possess. Top of the list is longevity, which means living to a mature old age.

This is followed by good fortune, which includes wealth and social status.

The third kind of luck is peace. This means enjoying good health and having peace of mind.

The fourth kind of luck is having a kind nature and being magnanimous and calm.

The last kind is called, literally, 'a good end'. This refers to a person being able to predict when their time is coming to an end in their old age, without suffering, worries and any regrets in life.

The five kinds of luck are often represented symbolically by five bats. Although the bat 蝠 (fú) is not the most lovable animal, it has the same pronunciation as 福 (fú), meaning 'luck', and paintings of five bats are often used as decorations in the traditional home. This symbolizes 'the five kinds of luck arriving at the door' 五福临门 (wǔ fú lín mén).

flowers 花 huā

Most countries have a national flower. China has yet to decide officially on its national flower. The choice seems to be between the plum blossom and the peony.

plum blossom

peony

In the Chinese language, flowers are often associated with women. On the positive side, they can evoke the beauty of a woman in some set phrases, for example 'with the features of a flower and a face like the moon' 花容月貌 (huā róng yuè mào). A 'school or college flower' 校花 (xiào huā) used to refer to the most beautiful female student in a school or college.

Flowers may sometimes convey a negative message, especially when used in conjunction with the willow 柳 (liǔ). For example, a red-light district is described in the Chinese language as a 'floral street and willow lane' 花街柳巷 (huā jiē liǔ xiàng).

Idioms and phrases

花朵 huā duǒ
flower

花好月圆 huā hǎo yuè yuán
a congratulatory phrase wishing a couple a blissful marriage

花花绿绿 huā huā lǜ lǜ
colourful

花天酒地 huā tiān jiǔ dì
indulgence in noisy drinking parties

花无百日红 huā wú bǎi rì hóng
literally 'no flowers bloom forever', reminding people that there's always an end to the good times

花心 huā xīn
literally 'flower heart'; unfaithful to one's wife or girlfriend

花言巧语 huā yán qiǎo yǔ
sweet but insincere words

four 四 sì

Although four 四 (sì) is twice of two, which is considered good, the number is generally believed to be unlucky. When it is pronounced in Mandarin or some other dialects, the number sounds like 'death' or 'to be dead' 死 (sǐ) .

Some people selecting new apartments tend to avoid the fourth level or addresses containing the number four. In some cases this number is deliberately omitted from lifts. Likewise, numbers such as 14, 24, 34, 44 and so on, are considered unlucky.

Car owners tend to avoid the number too, especially if it comes at the end of the number plate. It is said that some bus companies also avoid registering number plates that end in four.

Idioms and phrases

四处 sì chù

everywhere

四分五裂 sì fēn wǔ liè

(of an organization) disintegrating, divisive

四合院 sì hé yuàn

a compound in which houses surround a square courtyard. You can still see some in Beijing.

四海 sì hǎi

literally 'the four seas', meaning the whole world

四海为家 sì hǎi wéi jiā

to make your home wherever you may be

四海之内皆兄弟 sì hǎi zhī nèi jiē xiōng dì

peoples of the world are like brothers

四季 sì jì

the four seasons

四面 sì miàn

four sides

四面八方 sì miàn bā fāng

on all sides

四面楚歌 sì miàn chǔ gē

besieged on all sides

四声 sì shēng

the four intonations of Chinese pronunciation

四月 sì yuè

April

four great inventions
四大发明 sì dà fā míng

The ancient Chinese are known to have contributed four important scientific and technological inventions to world civilization. The first one was the invention of the compass. The earliest form appeared in the Warring States period more than 2,000 years ago and was made using a natural magnetic stone and shaped like a Chinese soup spoon. A finer and more accurate needle form came much later, probably in the Song dynasty.

The second invention was paper-making. The person who is usually credited with this invention was Cai Lun, a eunuch living during the Eastern Han dynasty. He improved on earlier techniques to produce a better-quality paper.

The third invention was printing. About 1,300 years ago, during the period of the Sui dynasty, woodblock printing was invented, making the printing of books much easier than the more rudimentary methods using bamboo slabs and silk. Buddhist monks were amongst the earliest to take advantage of this invention and started to print for distribution portraits of Buddhist personalities and sutras, such as the complete text of the *Diamond Sutra*.

The last great invention was gunpowder, which was first made in China more than 1,000 years ago. Its invention seems to have been connected with the experiments of the Taoists as they attempted to produce pills of immortality.

Later, the gunpowder was introduced to the West and used widely in cannons and gunboats in wars.

the four treasures of the study
文房四宝 wén fáng sì bǎo

Traditionally, a Chinese study is inseparable from the four items that are associated with calligraphy and painting: the brush, the ink-stick, paper and ink-stone.

The brush used for calligraphy or painting comes in different sizes and is made from different types of animal hair. Some people even cut the hair of their newborn babies to make brushes as souvenirs. It is said that these brushes will make the children excel in their studies when they grow up.

The ink-stick and ink-stone come as a pair; one cannot do without the other. They can be elaborately designed and are often decorated with carvings. For example, it is quite common to find 'the five kinds of luck' carved on the ink-stone.

The paper used for calligraphy or Chinese painting is a special kind of high quality rice paper. It absorbs ink from the brush very well, preventing it from smudging.

fox 狐狸 hú li

The Chinese view of the fox is quite unlike that in the West, where fox hunting was a blood sport characterized by the noise of pursuing hounds and hunters on horseback.

In Chinese legends, the creature has much more romantic associations as the fox was believed to have magical powers attained through hundreds of years of solitary cultivation.

Eventually, the fox reached a stage where it could transform itself into a human, usually in the form of a beautiful woman, who would then go out to tempt unwary young scholars. The Chinese phrase *hu mei* 狐媚 (hú mèi) is still used, in a derogatory way, to describe any sexy woman who tries to seduce a man.

To this day, when a married man falls for a younger and often more attractive woman, the younger woman will be accused of being a temptress or a 'fox spirit' 狐狸精 (hú li jīng) by the man's wife and relatives.

狐狸精!

狐狸精!

In Chinese mythology, a fox with nine tails was supposed to be an auspicious animal that had lived 1,000 years. It symbolized good fortune and the blessing of many children.

But in the writings of later dynasties, the nine-tailed fox was often depicted as crafty and evil and possessed the power to transform itself into a beautiful and seductive woman. In popular Chinese culture, it was said that Daji, the favourite concubine of the tyrant King Zhou of the Shang dynasty, was the transformation of a nine-tailed fox.

The fox is popularly known to be a sly animal that is full of tricks. There is a Chinese fable that tells how a fox deceives a tiger into believing that he is more feared by the animals of the forest than the tiger is. He asks the tiger to follow behind him and, sure enough, when the other animals see the tiger, they are all frightened and run away. The Chinese idiom 狐假虎威 (hú jiǎ hǔ wēi), literally 'the fox exploiting the tiger's awe', means to use one's powerful connections to bully others.

Idioms and phrases

狐狸尾巴 hú li wěi ba

 literally 'the fox's tail'. It was believed that though the fox could turn into a human, it was unable to hide its tail at times. So this phrase means 'to expose one's ulterior motive'.

狐群狗党 hú qún gǒu dǎng

 a derogatory phrase meaning a gang of bad people

狐疑 hú yí

 to be suspicious, like a fox

fu 符 fú

In the Chinese language, *fu* may refer to amulets, which are small objects that people wear or keep to ward off evil, especially in the past. These small objects could be a gem or a coin.

Fu could also come in the form of scribbled words that Taoist priests prescribed for those seeking their help and which were supposed to protect them from harm.

Such *fu* might be glued to the door, for example, to prevent evil spirits from entering the house. Or they might be burnt so that the ash could then be mixed with water and consumed by the sick.

Fu also means incantations, that is, words with magical power scribbled by Taoist priests and are intended to bring misfortune, or even death, to a person's enemies.

Such curses were usually hidden somewhere near the victim. The whole process was therefore carried out surreptitiously. This practice was common in the past as a means to do harm to one's enemies.

34

Fu, Lu and *Shou*

福禄寿 fú lù shòu

Fu, Lu and *Shou* are three Taoist deities representing, respectively, good fortune, prosperity and longevity. The pursuit of all three has been a chief Chinese preoccupation for generations. Statues of these deities are commonly found in both Chinese homes and public places.

The three deities are often depicted holding something that shows who they are. The deity of good fortune, *Fu*, holds a scroll bearing the word 福 (fú, fortune), as he is able to dispense good fortune to people. His blessings include peace, safety and male children. The deity of prosperity, *Lu*, holds a gold ingot 元宝 (yuán bǎo) because he is able to make people rich and successful. The deity of longevity, *Shou*, has a peach 寿桃 (shòu táo) in one hand and is able to give people long life.

In some goldsmith's shops, you can still buy gold-plated figurines of the three deities as a gift. The three deities are also a popular subject in Lunar New Year paintings in village homes in China.

Idioms and phrases

福气 fú qì

good fortune; the same as **福分** (fú fen)

福无双至, 祸不单行 fú wú shuāng zhì huò bù dān xíng

literally 'good fortune never appears in pairs and disaster never comes singly'; it never rains but it pours

寿比南山 shòu bǐ nán shān

The Chinese often compare longevity to the Mount Heng in the south, one of the five famous mountains in China.

寿辰 shòu chén

birthday (usually of an elderly person); the same as **寿诞** (shòu dàn)

寿礼 shòu lǐ

birthday gift (usually for an elderly person)

寿面 shòu miàn

birthday noodles (usually for an elderly person)

寿命 shòu mìng

the life of a person

寿终正寝 shòu zhōng zhèng qǐn

(usually of an elderly person) to die a natural death

full 满 mǎn

The Chinese word 满 (mǎn) means 'complete' or 'full'. The word has a symbolic meaning during the Lunar New Year in particular. The rice container, for example, should be filled to the brim, symbolizing abundance.

The Chinese believe that the moon on the fifteenth day of every month of the lunar calendar is a full moon. On the fifteenth day of the eighth month (Mid-Autumn), the moon is at its fullest and brightest.

A baby's first month 满月 (mǎn yuè, or 'full month') is an important occasion. The celebration includes distributing Chinese snacks and red eggs (hard-boiled eggs that are dyed red) to friends and relatives so that they too can share the joy.

However, 'fullness' is considered less desirable in matters of education or knowledge, for example, and is not to be encouraged. The Chinese have a proverb that says 满招损 (mǎn zhāo sǔn), 谦受益 (qiān shòu yì), which means, literally, 'if you think you know everything, you invite loss; if you are humble, you will benefit'.

Idioms and phrases

满分 mǎn fēn
full marks

满腹牢骚 mǎn fù láo sāo
full of complaints

满门 mǎn mén
the whole family

满面 mǎn miàn
the whole face

满面春风 mǎn miàn chūn fēng
a face that shows happiness

满腔热情 mǎn qiāng rè qíng
full of enthusiasm

满身 mǎn shēn
the whole body

满意 mǎn yì
fully satisfied, very pleased

满载 mǎn zài
fully loaded

满载而归 mǎn zài ér guī
(after a shopping spree, for example) to return home with a full load

满足 mǎn zú
fully contented; the same as **满意** (mǎn yì)

ghost 鬼 guǐ

In Chinese folk culture, after people died, those who had contributed to the country or done good to the people would be worshipped as gods, deities or immortals and live in heaven. Most people would, however, become spirits or ghosts after their death and live in the nether world.

The Chinese people would make offerings to both gods and ghosts at certain festivals. They would pray to the gods for their blessings, as well as to the ghosts hoping that they have enough to eat and not suffer in the nether world, so that they would not return to disturb the living.

In the 19th century, during the Qing dynasty, when China was humiliated at the hands of the West, the Chinese people referred to Westerners by the derogatory name 'foreign ghosts' 洋鬼子 (yáng guǐ zi). Those Chinese who helped or worked for Westerners, or adopted Western ways themselves, were often called 'pseudo-foreign ghosts' 假洋鬼子 (jiǎ yáng guǐ zi).

A more neutral term *lao wai* 老外 (lǎo wài) is commonly used in China to refer foreigners.

The word is also used to refer to people, sometimes humorously, who are greedy 贪心鬼 (tān xīn guǐ), gluttonous 贪吃鬼 (tān chī guǐ), drunkards 酒鬼 (jiǔ guǐ) or lechers 色鬼 (sè guǐ).

The Chinese novel *Strange Stories from a Chinese Studio* 《聊斋志异》 (liáo zhāi zhì yì) is probably the best-known collection of ghost stories. It was written in the 17th century by Pu Songling, during the reign of the Qing emperor Kang-xi.

Pu Songling

Idioms and phrases

鬼斧神工 guǐ fǔ shén gōng

extremely skilful craftsmanship

鬼怪 guǐ guài

ghosts and monsters

鬼鬼祟祟 guǐ guǐ suì suì

to do things in a sneaky way so that other people will not find out

鬼话连篇 guǐ huà lián piān

a pack of lies

鬼魂 guǐ hún

ghosts and spirits

鬼混 guǐ hùn

a phrase that describes a person in the company of shady characters

鬼脸 guǐ liǎn

to make faces

鬼门关 guǐ mén guān

gate of hell

鬼迷心窍 guǐ mí xīn qiào

used to describe, metaphorically, someone who is obsessed with something

鬼主意 guǐ zhǔ yì

literally 'evil ideas'; often used, humorously, to mean 'funny ideas'

gift-giving 送礼 sòng lǐ

The giving or exchanging of gifts is a common social practice amongst family members, friends and business associates all over the world. In China, the old saying 'You give me a peach and I reciprocate with a plum' 投桃报李 (tóu táo bào lǐ) dates back to the age of the *Classic of Poetry*, more than 2,500 years ago.

This practice has lasted until today and extends to all walks of life. For example, when someone comes back from overseas, it is common for them to bring back some local produce or souvenirs for their relatives or friends. Such a gift is generally known as a 'gift accompanying the hand' 伴手礼 (bàn shǒu lǐ).

Likewise, it is a common practice for a married daughter to give presents to her parents during such important festivals as the Lunar New Year or Mid-Autumn Festival.

The true tradition of gift-giving involves the giving or receiving of relatively inexpensive presents. This is in line with the original concept that although a gift is small, the thought behind it is profound 礼轻情意重 (lǐ qīng qíng yì zhòng).

However, the practice of gift-giving is so pervasive that it is thought to be the root cause of corruption that has persisted throughout Chinese history. In imperial China, it was not uncommon for those who had the money (especially business people) to give very expensive presents to people in authority.

ginger 姜 jiāng

Ginger is one of the most important vegetables in Chinese cooking. It is often cut into thin slices and placed in hot oil before adding other ingredients.

In Chinese cooking, ginger often plays a supporting role; it is rarely eaten as a main dish. In the case of the month-long confinement after a woman delivers her baby, a common food for the mother is pig's trotters stewed with old ginger, sugar and vinegar. This recipe is believed to restore a woman's vitality and to remove the 'wind' left inside her after giving birth to the child.

As old ginger is known to be hotter than young ones, the Chinese use a phrase 姜是老的辣 (jiāng shì lǎo de là) as a compliment to an experienced older person who knows more than their younger colleagues, who may be well-educated but lack the necessary experience.

There is also a Chinese saying that local ginger is not as hot as foreign ginger 本地姜不辣 (běn dì jiāng bú là). The saying, usually voiced either out of jealousy or frustration, means that a local talent is less valued than an imported one. This means very much the same as another old saying: 'the foreign moon is rounder than the local one' 外国月亮比本地的圆 (wài guó yuè liàng bǐ běn dì de yuán).

ginseng 人参 rén shēn

In East Asia, China and Korea in particular, it is believed that ginseng is good for the body and can be taken regularly for good health. It is highly valued for its medicinal properties.

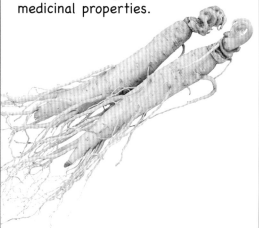

Some ginseng resembles the shape of a baby, with a 'body' and 'limbs'. There used to be a popular belief that one had to be very quiet and alert when approaching the plant before digging it up, lest it run away.

In China, Mount Changbai in the northeast is well known for its ginseng. Korea is known for its Korean ginseng and the United States too is noted for the American ginseng.

sliced American ginseng

Visitors to Korea will have noticed the many restaurants that sell ginseng chicken. This is a very popular dish with locals and tourists alike.

goat 羊 yáng

The Chinese word 羊 (yáng) is a generic term for a goat or sheep. The animal is considered auspicious because it sounds like the character 祥 (xiáng) that means 'luck'.

The goat is one of the 12 animals of the Chinese zodiac. In the Year of the Goat, instead of saying 三阳开泰 (sān yáng kāi tài), meaning 'the coming of spring', which brings with it good luck to the world, some people change the phrase to 三羊开泰, since the words 羊 (yáng) and 阳 (yáng) sound exactly the same.

There is a story about goats concerning Su Wu, an official in the Western Han period more than 2,000 years ago. He was an imperial envoy to the land of Xiongnu (Huns) on the western border of the Han Empire. The king of Xiongnu admired Su Wu's talent and attempted to persuade him to submit to his rule, but without success. So Su Wu was eventually exiled by the Xiongnu king to what is now Lake Baikal, with a herd of goats.

In Chinese culture, Su Wu was a role model of loyalty and honour. His life in the land of Xiongnu probably inspired many like-minded officials in later generations to emulate his sacrifice.

Idioms and phrases

羊毛　yáng máo
  wool

羊毛出在羊身上　yáng máo chū zài yáng shēn shang
  literally 'wool comes from the goat or lamb', meaning there's no free lunch – you eventually pay for what you are given

羊排　yáng pái
  lamb steak

羊皮　yáng pí
  the skin of a goat

羊绒　yáng róng
  cashmere

羊肉　yáng ròu
  mutton

god of wealth 财神 cái shén

The god of wealth is a deity commonly worshipped by the Chinese in the hope that he will bring wealth to the family. Belief in the god of wealth seems to have begun in the Song Dynasty, when commerce started to develop and people experienced the benefits associated with wealth.

The god of wealth is often depicted as a figure wearing a red robe (since red is a lucky colour to the Chinese). He has a long beard and an approachable demeanour. A handful of legendary or historical figures were formerly worshipped as gods of wealth. These included Fan Li, who lived during the Warring States period; Zhao Gongming, who was said to be from the Qin Dynasty, and his four subordinates; and even Guan Gong, who lived in the Three Kingdoms period.

An important tradition celebrated by many ordinary people is 'welcoming the god of wealth'. In northern China, people used to welcome him on the Lunar New Year's Eve. Someone in the family would stand outside the house holding a bundle of firewood 柴(chái), which sounds similar to 财 (cái), meaning wealth, and then dash into the living room. This represented 'wealth' coming into the house.

In southern China, people used to mark the ceremony on the eve of the fourth day of the Lunar New Year with the lighting of firecrackers and the making of offerings to the god, since the following day was said to be his birthday. During the ceremony, some people offered a large carp 鲤(lǐ), which sounds like 利(lì), meaning 'profit', to the god. When the head and tail of the fish curled up, it looked like an ingot, which was used as money in ancient China. All this represented good fortune.

Even today, the tradition of 'welcoming the god of wealth' continues to be observed. During the Lunar New Year, someone will dress up as the god of wealth, in red robe, and goes around the neighbourhood to distribute sweets wrapped in the shape of coins and wish people good fortune.

Idioms and phrases

财　cái

wealth

财宝　cái bǎo

money and valuables

财产　cái chǎn

property, asset

财大气粗　cái dà qì cū

literally 'a person who is very rich tends to speak louder'

财富　cái fù

wealth

财迷心窍　cái mí xīn qiào

crazy about money

财运　cái yùn

one's luck in making money

财主　cái zhǔ

a person who has lots of money

god of longevity 寿星 shòu xīng

The god of longevity is often depicted as a short, kind, old man with a long white flowing beard. He is usually accompanied by such symbols of longevity as the deer, crane and a large peach. He also has a distinct bulging forehead and a pair of large ears. All these are believed to be symbols of long life and make him stand out among the deities.

He is a legendary deity in Taoist mythology, depicted alongside such figures as the god of fortune and the god of prosperity.

Today when an elderly man celebrates his birthday, he is often referred to as the 'god of longevity' 寿星公 (shòu xīng gōng).

gold 金 jīn

Gold has been valued in the East since time immemorial and is widely used in ornaments and jewellery. When a wedding takes place, for example, items made of gold are almost always given to the bride by her mother and mother-in-law.

Gold has great cultural significance. For example, the Chinese phrase 'a house made of gold to house A Jiao' 金屋藏娇 (jīn wū cáng jiāo) has its origin in a Han dynasty story, which relates how Emperor Wu-ti, when young, became infatuated with a girl called A Jiao and offered to marry her and build her a house of gold.

A burial suit made of pieces of jade tied together with gold thread was worn by several Han dynasty emperors and their consorts when they died.

In China, gold has traditionally been equated with jade, and the two words often appear together in phrases, for example 金玉良言 (jīn yù liáng yán), meaning 'advice as valuable as gold and jade'.

In the past, the list of successful candidates at the imperial exams was known as the 'golden imperial notice' or 金榜 (jīn bǎng). Some phrases with the word gold are still in use today: a bright future is referred to as a 'golden road' 金光大道 (jīn guāng dà dào); a magnificent building may 'radiate golden and green light' 金碧辉煌 (jīn bì huī huáng); and a singer with a sweet voice is said to have a 'golden voice' 金嗓子 (jīn sǎng zi).

People also like to use the word gold when referring to certain Chinese zodiac animal signs, thus emphasizing the auspicious quality of the animal in question. For example, the Chinese may refer to the rooster as Golden Rooster, the goat as Golden Goat and the ox as Golden Ox.

Other than being a precious metal, gold is often associated with the winner in a competition or tournament. For example, the gold medal is awarded to the champion of a sporting event.

During the Ming and Qing dynasties, the phrase 千金 (qiān jīn, 'a thousand taels of gold') appeared frequently in novels, usually in reference to someone's daughter. Today, when you want to be formal, you can still use the term in the same way.

Idioms and phrases

金币 jīn bì
gold coin

金橘 jīn jú
kumquat

金库 jīn kù
treasury; the phrase can be used metaphorically to refer to someone's banker

金钱 jīn qián
money

金色 jīn sè
gold colour

金属 jīn shǔ
metals

金条 jīn tiáo
gold bars

金玉满堂 jīn yù mǎn táng
literally 'gold and jade filling the whole hall of the house', meaning very rich

金字招牌 jīn zì zhāo pái
literally 'the signboard of a shop written in golden letters', meaning to make a boastful claim of one's own product

good fortune 福 fú

Fortune or luck is particularly important to the Chinese. Some people even believe that it is better to be born lucky than rich.

$1,000,000

Some people seek to improve their fortune by hanging the word 福 (fú) upside down, especially during the Lunar New Year. The upside-down 福 (fú) or 福倒 (fú dào) (倒 means 'upside-down') sounds similar to 福到 (fú dào) (到 means 'arrive'), meaning 'luck has arrived (in the house)'.

You usually wish the elderly good fortune and longevity on their birthday. It is traditional to wish them that their fortune be as extensive and deep as the great sea in the east 福如东海 (fú rú dōng hǎi) and that their life be long like the mountain in the south 寿比南山 (shòu bǐ nán shān). While the sea in the east need not necessarily refer to any particular sea, it is believed that the mountain in the south refers to the Mount Heng in Hunan province, one of the five famous mountains of China.

gourd 葫芦 hú lu

The gourd is a fruit that looks rather like a bottle with a rounded bottom. When it is young, its flesh can be eaten. When it is ripe, the outer shell is often used as a container. As the mouth of the gourd is very small, it is not easy to know what is inside. Consequently, the expression 不知他葫芦里卖的是什么药 (bù zhī dào tā hú lu lǐ mài de shì shén me yào) , literally 'not knowing what medicine he's selling in his gourd', means not knowing what someone is up to.

The magical gourd makes many appearances in Chinese fantasy fiction. For example, in *Journey to the West*, Sun Wukong is once trapped inside a gourd by demons. Of course, he is smart enough to escape.

In Chinese popular culture, the 'itinerant monk' Ji Gong is depicted holding a gourd containing wine in one hand and a torn fan in the other. He uses his magical power to help the poor and punish the wicked.

Amongst the Eight Immortals, the limping Li Tieguai uses a gourd as his magical weapon.

46

the Great Wall of China
长城 cháng chéng

The Great Wall of China took over 2,000 years to build, starting in the Spring and Autumn period of Chinese history more than 2,500 years ago. It stretches from Shanhai Pass in the east, runs along the northern borders of the country, and ends in the west – a total length of about 5,000 km.

After he unified China, the First Emperor of the Qin dynasty, Qin Shi Huang, linked many of the individual walls constructed by different states. But the major work was done much later, only during the Ming dynasty.

There is a popular story about a woman called Meng Jiangnu and the Great Wall. According to one version, during the Qin dynasty, Qin Shi Huang used forced labour to construct the wall. Shortly after their marriage, the husband of Meng Jiangnu was conscripted to build the wall and never returned.

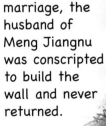

When Meng Jiangnu went to the site to search for her husband, she was told that he had died of hard labour. She then searched for his dead body but could not find it and burst into tears. Her heartbroken sobs were heard in heaven and in the end the wall collapsed. In Chinese folklore, this is known as 'Meng Jiangnu brings down the Great Wall with her cry' 孟姜女哭倒长城 (mèng jiāng nǚ kū dǎo cháng chéng).

The Great Wall played an important role in keeping the 'barbarian' invaders from frequent distuebance to people living inside the wall in the history.

When astronauts orbited in space around the earth, it was said that some could see the Great Wall with the naked eye, but others said this was impossible. Despite this controversy, the Great Wall remains an architectural achievement of the ancient world.

green 青 qīng

In the past, the word 青 (qīng) means not only green, but also black and blue, depending on the context. For example, 青布 (qīng bù) meant black cloth, and 青丝 (qīng sī, literally 'green silk') described the long black hair of a woman. In order to avoid confusion, the word 绿 (lù) was introduced later, meaning green.

In the past, brothels were called 青楼 (qīng lóu), meaning 'blue building', and 青楼女子 (qīng lóu nǚ zǐ), literally 'a girl from the blue building', referred to a prostitute.

In the Chinese language, there are a number of examples in which the colour 青 means blue. For example, the saying 青出于蓝而胜于蓝 (qīng chū yú lán ér shèng yú lán), literally means that 'blue originates from the indigo plant, but is bluer than the plant itself'. It is often used to refer to a pupil who is more outstanding than their teacher.

Idioms and phrases

青菜 qīng cài

(green) vegetables

青草 qīng cǎo

grass

青春 qīng chūn

the prime of one's life; youth

不分青红皂白 bù fēn qīng hóng zào bái

one does not care whether something is right or wrong

青黄不接 qīng huáng bù jiē

a temporary shortage of something

青年 qīng nián

young man

青山 qīng shān

green hills or blue mountains

青山绿水 qīng shān lǜ shuǐ

(of a beautiful landscape) blue mountains and green waters

青少年 qīng shào nián

youngsters

青蛙 qīng wā

frog

青云直上 qīng yún zhí shàng

a phrase that is often used to describe someone's meteoric rise;
the same as **平步青云** (píng bù qīng yún)

Guan-yin 观音 guān yīn

The pictures or statues of Guan-yin that we see today are those of a female, and she is generally identified as being a goddess. However, before the Song Dynasty, people apparently believed that Guan-yin was in fact a male who transformed himself into a female in order to rescue people from suffering and distress.

According to one source, Guan-yin was originally called Princess Miaoshan, the third daughter of a legendary king. Miaoshan was by nature a kind person and always helped those in need. She was so devoted to Buddhism that she later decided to become a nun.

Popularly known as the Goddess of Mercy, Guan-yin was noted for her compassion and became one of the most popular deities in Buddhist mythology.

Today, her statues, almost all in white, may be seen in many places. Some women believe that the White Guan-yin answers their prayers for baby boys, hence the saying 'Guan-yin sending a son' 观音送子 (guān yīn sòng zǐ).

Guan Yu 关羽 guān yǔ

Guan Yu (also known as Guan Yunchang), Liu Bei and Zhang Fei were household names all living in the Three Kingdoms period, in the third century AD. Their stories have been vividly told in the novel *Romance of the Three Kingdoms*.

Living in turbulent times, the trio decided to become sworn brothers and performed the ceremony in a peach garden. This paved the way for similar practice amongst people who shared the same aspirations. Guan Yu ranked second in terms of age, after Liu Bei.

The popular novel depicts Guan Yu as being tall, with a red face and a long beautiful beard. His battle horse was the 'red-rabbit horse' 赤兔马 (chì tù mǎ) and with his favourite weapon, the 'green dragon crescent-moon sabre' 青龙偃月刀 (qīng lóng yǎn yuè dāo), he won many battles.

Besides his bravery and righteousness, Guan Yu symbolized loyalty in folk culture. He was not only heavily relied upon by Liu Bei, but was also much respected by Liu's arch rival Cao Cao. Although Cao Cao tried to persuade Guan Yu to cross over to his camp, Guan Yu never wavered in his loyalty to Liu Bei.

After his death, Guan Yu became a folk hero and was widely known as Guan Gong 关公 (guān gōng) or Guan Di 关帝 (guān dì) and was even worshipped as a god. People throughout China built temples to house his portrait or statue.

hat 帽子 mào zi

The Chinese first adopted the custom of wearing hats (called 冠 guān in the past) thousands of years ago. The hats of the ordinary people were usually made of cloth and coloured black. The hats of scholars were lighter in colour.

In the old days, when boys reached the age of 20 they had to perform a hat ceremony, called 加冠礼 (jiā guān lǐ).

In the case of girls, when they reached the age of 15, their hair had to be bound up and held in place with a pin. This was known as 及笄礼 (jí jī lǐ). Both ceremonies signified adulthood and the fact that they had reached marriageable age.

The style of hats varied under succeeding dynasties, but the hat ceremony remained important. In the modern era the hat, or cap, for men has assumed a more practical function, mainly to shade the wearer from the sun. For women, the hat has become not just a piece of clothing but also a fashion item.

Visitors to China should be aware that while it is perfectly acceptable to wear any style of hat or cap they choose, they should never wear a green hat 戴绿帽 (dài lǜ mào) . This is because a green hat in Chinese culture means the wearer is a cuckold whose wife has had an affair with another man.

Appendix:

Chronological Table of the Chinese Dynasties

The Paleolithic Period	Approx. 1,700,000–10,000 years ago
The Neolithic Age	Approx. 10,000–4,000 years ago
Xia Dynasty	2070–1600 BC
Shang Dynasty	1600–1046 BC
Western Zhou Dynasty	1046–771 BC
Spring and Autumn Period	770–476 BC
Warring States Period	475–221 BC
Qin Dynasty	221–206 BC
Western Han Dynasty	206 BC–AD 25
Eastern Han Dynasty	25–220
Three Kingdoms	220–280
Western Jin Dynasty	265–317
Eastern Jin Dynasty	317–420
Northern and Southern Dynasties	420–589
Sui Dynasty	581–618
Tang Dynasty	618–907
Five Dynasties	907–960
Northern Song Dynasty	960–1127
Southern Song Dynasty	1127–1279
Yuan Dynasty	1206–1368
Ming Dynasty	1368–1644
Qing Dynasty	1616–1911
The Republic of China	1912–1949
The People's Republic of China	Founded in 1949

Note

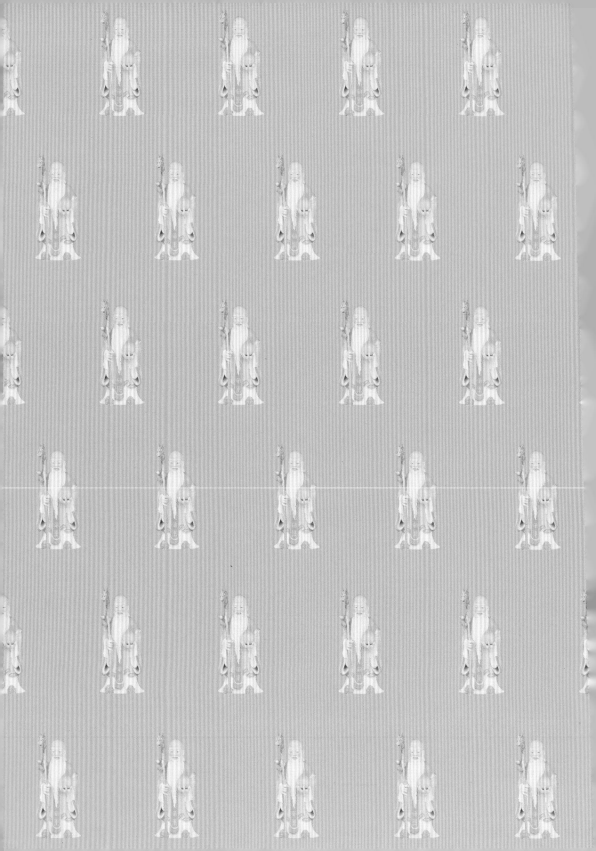